Rainy Day Kids
ADVENTURE
BOOK

Rainy Day Kids

ADVENTURE

BOOK

Steph Scott and katie Akers

BATSFORD

To Allan, KT's Pa, without whom none
of this would ever have happened.
S.S.

To Pa.
K.A.

First published in the United Kingdom in 2017 by
Batsford
43 Great Ormond Street
London
WC1N 3HZ

An imprint of Pavilion Books Company Ltd
Copyright © Pavilion Books Company Ltd 2017
Text and illustrations copyright © Steph Scott and Katie Akers 2017

ISBN 978-1-84994-438-0

A CIP catalogue record for this book is available from the British Library.

10 9 8 7 6 5 4 3 2 1

Reproduction by Mission Productions Ltd, Hong Kong
Printed and bound by Toppan Leefung Printing Ltd, China

This book can be ordered direct from the publisher at www.pavilionbooks.com

Distributed in the United States and Canada by Sterling Publishing Co., Inc.,
1166 Avenue of the Americas, 17th Floor, New York, NY 10036, USA

CONTENTS

Deep in the woods there's **a place that shines**.
A place that only you can find.
A place where **magic is written** in the trees.
Upon the **dew** and the **gentle breeze**.
There are flowers, **streams** and **real-life dreams**,
dragons dodging **bright sunbeams**.

It's a place you are **brave** and **quick** and **smart**,
where you can hear nature's **beating heart**.
There's so much to hear
and say and do.
Go and find it,
it's waiting **just for you**.

INTRODUCTION

Welcome back to you all: children, parents, grandparents, uncles, aunts, teachers, forest-school leaders and childminders, and to all flora and fauna everywhere, this time joined by all things weathery. Just as in our previous book, *Let's Go Outside*, whether you are already passionate about nature and the outdoors or are just taking your first steps out into a rainy day adventure, you are very welcome. This book is written for you all.

The Rainy Day Kids Adventure Book is the second in our series of activity books for children aged 3–99 years. It is all about weather. The rainy stuff, the windy stuff and all that stuff that comes along when it's really cold outside. Other books focus on all the wonderful things you can do indoors when it's wet or chilly, but this one's about what you can do *outdoors*! So shout 'Yippee!', put on your mac, pull on your wellies and run outside. A marvellous, multi-sensory adventure playground awaits you.

THE OUT PACK

Just as in our first book, *Let's Go Outside*, all our ideas truly come to life when you also have the Out Pack. It's the other bit that you need to make the magic happen. The Out Pack is your child's own special backpack containing all the bits and pieces required to complete the activities, in addition to a few items that they can easily forage from nature. Your child's Out Pack is any bag that's comfy for them to wear and can hold everything they need. You might want to think about getting a backpack that is waterproof, for obvious reasons!

What your child might choose to do today depends only on their mood, the season, the weather and how much outdoor space and time

is available. Together you could make a Mr Snowman Head (page 122) or fly a woven kite (page 77). You could find out how the rain is made or where the wind comes from.

As long as you know a cloud from a breeze and an ice flake from a puddle, you're ready for some adventures.

WHAT'S IN THE OUT PACK?

All the items in the Out Pack are easy to find and cheap to buy. You may already have some of them at home. Be sure to keep it well stocked so you don't run out of any essentials while you're out and about. This is a list of what we keep in our Out Packs...

☐ **This book!**

☐ **Coloured pens**

☐ **Masking tape** You won't need anything thicker than 12mm wide

☐ **Wool** You can get two balls of different colours, a multi-coloured ball or just a ball of your favourite colour

☐ **Plastic-coated garden wire** You can buy this in a reel with a safe cutter from anywhere that sells garden supplies

☐ **Elastic bands** Flat elastic bands of many colours are useful

☐ **Paperclips**

☐ **Ball of string**

☐ **Wooden beads** Big and small, bumpy and smooth

☐ **Child-friendly scissors** They must be able to cut string

A SMALL NOTE

The Rainy Day Kids Adventure Book and
the Out Pack are intended for interactive
adventures outdoors. Children will need your
help and supervision with many parts of the
creative process. We recommend that when
the Out Pack is open, there is an adult nearby
to lend a hand. When your child's Out Pack
is at home and not being played with, it is best
placed in a high spot out of their reach. There
are items in there that children need a helping
hand with, and we're sure that you'd rather
not wind that ball of string up again and again
and again!

HOW TO FORAGE

Foraging is a wonderful skill that will help your child with every part of their Out Pack experience. It is basically about searching and finding. Kids love to pick up bits and pieces from nature, so they're likely very accomplished foragers already. In a nutshell, it's about helping your child to search for and find whatever they might be looking for, and it's especially about helping them to know what is okay to take from nature. It's about gathering this up and discovering not only how incredible all these treasures are, but also the wonderful things that we can make with them.

Foraging is a long walk for the perfect stick – it's finding the sycamore pod that flies best and knowing when you've found a weeping willow and how it can help you make a million and one things.

WET, WINDY AND FROSTY FORAGING!

It's fun to forage whatever the weather. When it's windy you can forage things as they float past you in the breeze! But it is also fun to be able to make your rainy, windy, snowy creations as soon as the weather rolls in. So perhaps you could keep a box of sticks and nature bits in your house and then you can get Out Packing straight away. And while we do want you to get out in wet, windy and cold days, it's important not to stay out for too long. Numb little fingers can't tie knots!

Most of the creations in *The Rainy Day Kids Adventure Book* can be made with bits and pieces from nature that can be found on the ground. You will, however, also find that there are a handful of creations that require foraging items from nature that are still living. These may be a few wild flowers from a lawn or meadow, a short stick of elder wood, a green leaf from a luscious hedge or a willow shoot.

We have specifically chosen trees and plants that are known to be robust, quick growers that are abundant throughout the year. They are trees and plants that like to be pruned and can cope with us carefully taking small bits from them. Having said that, if you find a willow tree that is looking a bit lacklustre, perhaps leave him until he appears a bit livelier.

HOW DOES IT ALL WORK?

The Rainy Day Kids Adventure Book and your Out Pack are designed for each other. The book has the ideas and the pack delivers the means to achieving them. All you need to do is decide what you are going to do today, go foraging for the bits you need from nature, take out whatever is required from your Out Pack and follow the instructions. The rest is down to your imagination.

WHAT IS AN OUTPACKER?

Outpackers can make an adventure out of any day. They know all about nature and how to take care of it. They also know how to stay warm, dry and safe. Use these rhymes and raps to help you as you take your first steps to becoming an Outpacker...

If it's made by nature it can stay,
if it's from the Out Pack take it away.

Berries, berries never pick
They can make you super-sick.

Fungi, fungi never touch
They could hurt you very much.

My stick is longer than my arm
If I wave it, it might do harm
Drag It, drag it, drag it...

Keep adventures right
on track
Don't get caught
without a snack.

Snow, wind, rain or shine
Weather changes all the time
Keep a mac inside your pack
And something spare to warm
your back.

Sticks in faces are no good
Keep them down, you know
you should
Watch it, watch it, watch it...

HOW TO REMEMBER YOUR SEASONS

It can be a bit tricky to remember the seasons, coming and going and going and coming all the time, and as we talk about them a lot in this book, we've made up a little rhyme to help you remember them. You can sing it to the tune of the nursery rhyme 'Twinkle, Twinkle, Little Star', or you can say it as a rap, or you can learn it just as it is. It goes like this:

Winter feels so very cold
In spring the little buds unfold
Summer's green all down the lane
Autumn all comes down again
Seasons come and then they go...
nature's dazzling magic show!

Let's go outside on a rainy day and **celebrate nature**, from the smallest backyard to the **largest wilderness**. Let's go outside, wherever you may be.

Let's have a rainy day **adventure and discover** the magic of plants, animals, seasons and weather. Let's **marvel at it all**.

Let's go out in the rain and imagine – kids **delight** in their little piece of **crafted nature** that can take them **to the moon and back**.

Let's go outside in the rain with the Out Pack ... Waterproofs, wellies, **Out Pack and go!**

RAIN

Rain, **rain**, don't go away,
Tell us that you'll **stay and play**.

Shower us with **cats and dogs**,
So we can play at **being frogs**.

Drizzling, **mizzling**, pelting down,
We **splash and splosh** … but not a frown.

Rain we're sorry, we were wrong,
You can stay here all day long!

TALKING ABOUT RAIN

Have you ever looked out of the window on a rainy day and heard someone say:

'Hooray, it's raining! Let's all go outside, to sing and dance in the rain!'

You've never heard that? Perhaps you're more used to hearing...

'Oh dear, it's raining.'

Or,
'What a gloomy day.'

Or,
'Isn't the weather grim?'

Or even,
'Oh, it's MISERABLE outside!'

Rainy weather gets called some horrible names. It's no wonder that when the clouds open and the raindrops fall, we feel like we ought to stay indoors and out of the wet!

When it's raining just a little bit we say it's SPITTING...that doesn't sound nice. Or when there's a misty sort of rain we say it's MIZZLING. Surely nothing sounds more miserable than that! Perhaps we need to get to know it a bit better.

Rain is water that falls from the clouds that float across our sky. Sometimes the clouds are thick, full and grey, and sometimes they are light and wispy, and can be all the colours of our rising or setting sun. Not all clouds are rain clouds, but one of our favourite rain clouds is the thick, grey blanket called the nimbostratus cloud. You can find out more about it and other clouds in the skills section, where we help you with your weather-guessing skills (page 148).

WHAT ARE CLOUDS MADE OF?

Clouds are made of lots and lots of teeny-tiny water droplets. Teeny-tiny water droplets that come together to float across our sky like puffs of candyfloss! But where do these teeny-tiny droplets come from? Think hard about where most of the water is on our planet…most of it's in our oceans and seas. Somehow some of the water from our oceans and seas gets up into the sky, but instead of having puddles in the sky, we have clouds. How does water get from the ocean and into the sky? The secret lies in how amazing water is. Water can be a totally different thing depending on how hot or cold it is…

When it's warmed up it turns into a gas, just like the steam that rises off your bubble bath. When it's very cold it's a solid, like ice lollies and snow. In between steam and ice, when it's not super-hot or super-cold, it is a liquid, like the water in streams, rivers and oceans.

HYDRO FLAME: WATER SUPERHERO!

If I could be a superhero, I would definitely
be Hydro Flame: half human, half alien from
the water planet, Aquaria! I would use water
power to protect the world and defeat evil by
changing from an invisible, super-hot gas to an
indestructible water force, and then to an ice-
cold frozen solid that turns you into a snowflake
if you touch me!

Can you find Hydro Flame and the three
water superpowers in your own experimental
laboratory (I mean, your kitchen!)? Have you got
any ice cubes in the fridge? And is there water in
the tap? And can you ask a grown-up to boil the
kettle to make steam?

THE WATER CYCLE

The water cycle is how water moves around our Earth, from the sky to the ground to the rivers and oceans and back again.

EVAPORATION

The water droplets that make the clouds started out as water vapour. How does that happen? The hot sun shines down on the oceans and seas that we sail on and dive into, and warms them up. Although we can't see it, some of the warmer top layer turns from liquid into water vapour that floats off as part of the air. This is called *evaporation.*

CONDENSATION

Another incredible thing about air is that when it gets warmer it rises and when it gets cooler it sinks. So the warm water vapour that comes off the cooler oceans and seas rises up, up, up in the warmer air, like a hot-air balloon. But then it meets cooler air way up in the sky, and the water vapour turns back into water, taking the form of millions and gazillions of teeny-tiny water droplets. And can you remember what millions and gazillions of teeny-tiny water droplets look like when they're in the sky? CLOUDS!

It's the same thing as when the window goes foggy when you have a bath, or when you can see your breath on a cold day. It's called *condensation.*

PRECIPITATION

Bit by bit these tiny water droplets come together, and start to make bigger droplets. Soon they become so big that they start falling to the ground, first a few and then more and more. This is called *precipitation*. But another name for it is RAIN!

COLLECTION

But this isn't the end of it. The rain makes puddles and streams that flow into rivers and lakes, which then flow out to sea. This last bit is called *collection*.

Can you imagine what might happen next? Well, it starts all over again! Water in the oceans becomes clouds and the clouds become rain and the rain becomes rivers and the rivers become oceans, again and again.

We call the whole thing the *WATER CYCLE*.

HOW IMPORTANT IS RAIN?

Rain is probably the most valuable and life-giving weather of all. If it didn't rain, our world wouldn't be able to survive. Along with the sun and the air, rain keeps our world happy and healthy. It brings water to all living things, including us. Water, clouds and rain, all neatly delivered to us by nature itself, and for free! Just imagine if it was the same with pizza!

Water is life! For us humans it is as important as the air we breathe. Without it, we simply cannot survive. It is hard for people to live in the deserts of our world because there is little water to drink, and it is extremely hard to grow food without water. The people who do live in deserts or other very dry places spend a lot of time hoping for rain. They may have to travel a long way to get water from a river or stream.

In countries that have lots of rain the plants and trees are lush and green, crops grow well and nobody has to worry about having enough water to drink. But often there's a lot of moaning about the weather! 'If only it wasn't raining!'

But really we should be dancing in the rain, and singing about how this precious water brings life, food, growth and happiness. What's more, if you're dressed up and ready to enjoy them, those 'gloomy', 'miserable' rainy days can be full of adventures.

It just takes different ways of:

Thinking about them
Talking about them
Preparing for them
And going outside to enjoy them.

RULES FOR ENJOYING RAIN

1 DON'T GET TOO WET. Wear the right clothes.

2 DON'T MIND GETTING WET (once you're wearing the right clothes)

3 DON'T STAY OUT IN IT FOR TOO LONG (especially if you're feeling cold or damp)

4 TALK POSITIVELY ABOUT RAINY DAYS. Don't call them miserable or gloomy, or you won't enjoy them!

Find your waterproofs.
Put on your wellies.
Let's go outside,
it's time to sing and dance in the rain!

WHAT SHALL I WEAR?

This bit is the most important of all. Without the right clothes, you can end up cold and wet and wanting nothing more than to get out of it. But with the right clothes, a rainy day is special. Rain changes the world in a way you can only discover when you're feeling dry and warm and invincible. You will need:

- Wellies
- A raincoat or mac
- Waterproof trousers

On a rainy day in summer you can wear wellies, a raincoat and shorts. Skin is wonderfully waterproof and will dry out in a jiffy. In winter, you might like some extra layers underneath your waterproofs. Some warm waterproof ski gloves can make all the difference. And please check that mums and dads or other grown-ups have got the right clothes on as well. They might need more persuading to go outdoors when it's raining, so give them plenty of encouragement!

Look, it's raining. Hooray! Try saying it and you might start to believe it!

RAIN CHECKLIST

☁ Listen to the sound rain makes.

☁ Look at how rain changes the world around us.

☁ Taste it. Go on, stick your tongue out and taste.

☁ Smell it. Are you standing on grass or mud, or are you on the pavement? Does rain change the way the world smells?

☁ Touch it. Drip drop, drip drop. On your face and on your hands.

☁ Enjoy it!

RAIN QUICKIES

Getting used to being out in the rain and learning to love it might take a bit of time, especially for mums and dads and other grown-ups! So here are a few quick rain activities. You can pop outside and play for a short time and then pop back inside again! One of the very best things about rain is puddles. Sometimes there are puddles scattered the whole way down the pavement or the muddy path. Here is some puddle fun that you can have as you start out on your adventures.

PUDDLE POUNCE

How many puddles can you count? Spot as many as you can. Can you jump from one puddle to another? How far can you get?

Sometimes when the sun comes out, there will be wet bits and dry bits of pavement. Can you jump over the puddles from one dry bit to the next? You can do this one even if you haven't got your wellies on.

PUDDLE TARGETS

Drop a big leaf, a rock or piece of wood into a puddle to make a target. Collect some tiny stones and throw them to try to hit your targets. Smaller leaves can have more points than bigger ones. Be careful to pick a puddle away from people or anything valuable.

SINK AND FLOAT

Forage for lots of different nature stuff. Collect stuff that's fluffy, seedy, hard, soft, light, big and small. Find a big puddle and put things in it. Can you guess which will float and which will sink?

PUDDLE OLYMPICS

Long jump, steeplechase, high jump, hurdles…Can you jump puddles to create your own Olympic Games?

FOOTPRINTS

Once your boots are nice and wet, find a sunny dry patch to make footprints in. Can you make a wet welly trail, or arrows for your friends to follow, or perhaps even make a picture on the ground? You could use welly footprints to make a flower, a smiley face, a sun – or even a wellysaurus! How long do the footprints last before the sun dries them up?

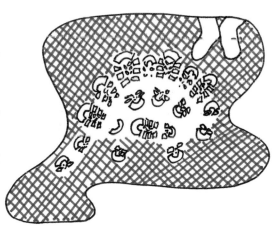

GRANNY'S WELLY STEPS

The object of the game is to get Granny wet by jumping in the puddle next to her!

1 The person who is going to be Granny stands in front of a big puddle, facing away from everyone else. The others stand at the starting point, 15 big steps away and looking towards Granny. Put a stick on the ground to remember where the starting point is.

2 Once the game starts, everyone slowly creeps up on Granny and tries to splash into the puddle next to her before she catches them.

3 Granny needs to listen really carefully. If she hears anyone creeping up on her, she turns around really quickly.

4 When Granny turns around everyone must stand really still. If Granny spots anyone moving, that person must return to the starting stick and start all over again.

5 The player who jumps in the puddle next to Granny first is the winner, and gets to be the next Granny.

34

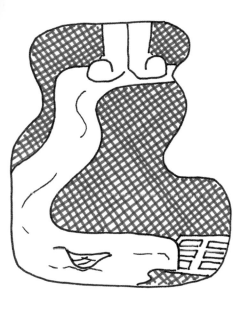

RAIN EXPLORATION

Sometimes so much rain falls from the sky. Then where does it all go? Follow it. Can you see the streams of rainwater at the sides of the roads? Take a tiny leaf or a bit of a big leaf and send it down the stream. Where does it go? Can you follow it the whole way to a drain? Watch the water gurgle and froth.

DRIP DASH

Trees love rain. They make a good shelter apart from the odd drip on the top of your head. Can you run under a big tree without getting dripped on? We call this a drip dash.

TREE DOWNPOUR

Gently shake a tree that's been rained on to make a mini downpour. As a bit of a practical joke, you could invite someone to join you under the tree before you shake. 'Hey, come and look over here. Ha! Tree downpour!'

RAIN SAFARI

It's not only the flowers, trees and plants that change when the rain falls. Many little birds, insects and other animals like to come out and play when it's raining. Can you see or hear any on your rain safari?

MUD MAKE-UP

Rain makes the mud like wet finger-paint. What will your tribe look like? Will you have mud stripes on your cheeks or spots on your forehead? Don't worry, it all washes off.

PUDDLE PONY

A puddle pony is a chunky stick with personality! It's the very best companion on a puddly day.

COLLECT TOGETHER

From nature
- ☐ 1 chunky stick

From the Out Pack
- ☐ Garden wire
- ☐ 2 beads
- ☐ Wool
- ☐ Scissors
- ☐ String

HOW TO MAKE IT

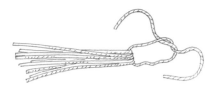

1 To make the eyes, cut a piece of garden wire about two grown-up hand-lengths long. Thread two beads onto the middle and fix them in place with a pinch and twist of the wire.

2 Wrap the wire around one end of your stick. This is your pony's head. Secure the wire to the stick with a tight pinch and twist.

3 For the tail, cut a three-arm's-length of wool and wind it round and round in a loop that is about a hand's-length long, or longer if you want a swishy tail. There will be loops at both ends.

4 Cut another arm's-length of wool and thread it through the loops at one end. Tie a double knot to secure it and leave two long ends. Then cut through all the loops at the other end to make a bushy tail.

5 Wrap the long ends a few times around your pony and tie on the tail with another double knot.

6 Cut a piece of string of about one arm's length.

7 Tie a fish-on-a-dish knot (clove hitch) just behind your pony's eyes to make its bridle (see skills section, page 140).

8 Perhaps try out your pony's showjumping skills with a few spectacular splash fences. Giddy up!

PUDDLE PAINTING

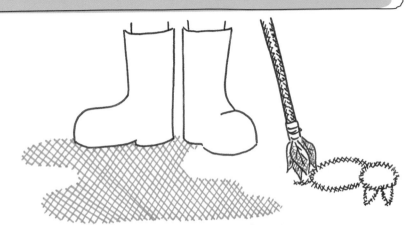

Take your magic paintbrush, dip it into a puddle, and use your imagination to paint amazing things. You can make it from grass or fern bristles, or anything bristly will do the trick.

If you mash grass into your puddle, do you get green paint? Does stamping your muddy wellies in the puddle make brown paint? Can you find anything else to make different colour puddle paints?

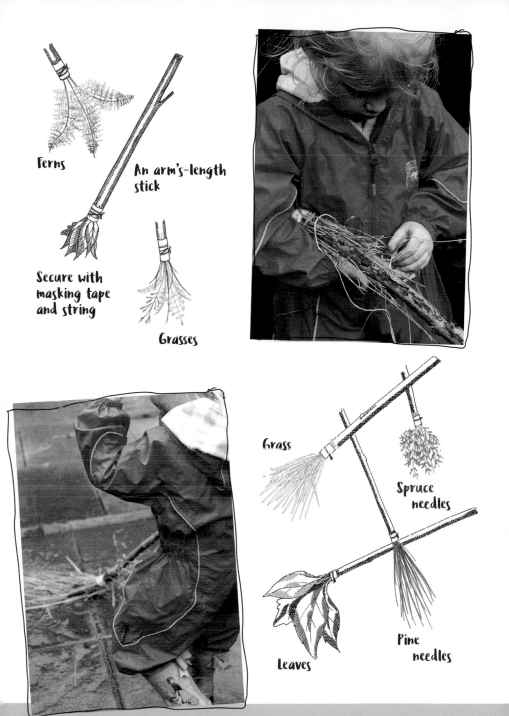

Ferns

An arm's-length stick

Secure with masking tape and string

Grasses

Grass

Spruce needles

Leaves

Pine needles

WATER WHEEL

Let's make an actual working water wheel. In olden times the flow of the river would push the wheel to grind the wheat to make the flour to make bread. See how your water wheel turns in the flow. Try it under the tap, in a gutter stream or under your water run (page 48). Is yours for making flour? Or just for rainy fun?

COLLECT TOGETHER

From nature

☐ 6 acorn cups – either double acorn cups or single ones with a bit of twig still attached
☐ 3 hand-length sticks

From the Out Pack

☐ Garden wire
☐ String
☐ Scissors
☐ 2 beads

HOW TO MAKE IT

1 Attach a hand-length of garden wire to each acorn cup with a pinch and twist, leaving two ends to secure to your sticks.

2 Take a stick and attach an acorn cup (or a pair) to each end, with one facing up and the other facing down.

3 Repeat for the other two sticks.

4 Using string, lash two sticks into a cross (see skills section, page 142), making sure the acorn cups are all facing in the same direction.

5 Lash the final stick on, making sure that its acorn cups are also facing in the same direction as the others.

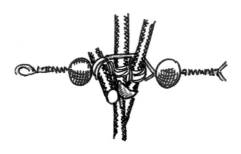

6 Cut half an arm's-length of garden wire and bend it in half. Twist the looped end until you have a finger's-length of twisted wire.

7 Take the loose ends of wire over the lashing and secure with a pinch and twist. Adjust and twist the wire until it's the same length on both sides.

8 Thread two beads on the end of each twisted wire to make two handles. Are all the acorn cups facing in the same direction as they go round the wheel?

9 Test your water wheel under a tap or stream. Your stick wheel should go round as the water fills the cups.

10 You can use masking tape to attach your beads to sticks and push these into the ground so your wheel is hanging just above the ground. It will work now under your watering can or hose.

FAIRY AND ELF POOL AND SPA

The garden fairies and elves are going to love this beautiful stone and leaf pool, freshly filled by rain from nimbostratus clouds. You can add the finest wooden sunbeds and hand-picked acorn cups, such luxury!

COLLECT TOGETHER

From nature

☐ 1 big stick
☐ Lots of leaves and stones; choose different thicknesses and sizes
☐ Mud

HOW TO MAKE IT

1 Use a big stick to dig a pit for your pool. Any shape you like, but keep it small and fairy-sized!

2 Lay half of your leaves inside the pool, covering as much as possible.

3 Choose little stones and lay them over the leaves.

4 To stop your pool from leaking, put some of the mud from digging your pit on top of the stones.

5 Cover this with the rest of your leaves. You can use bigger stones to push them down.

6 Now you can fill your pool with water from the tap. Or you could put one or more water runs (see page 48) around the pool to fill it from the rain.

7 Let the fairies and elves know that the pool is open!

Spa bed

1 Lash five sticks together to make a bed.

2 Attach a leg to each corner using string.

3 Add a moss pillow.

Table Flat stone or bark resting on stones.

Jug Bead threaded with garden wire handle.

Magazine Leaf cut into a square. Use a pen to add cover.

Cup Acorn cup with garden wire handle.

Flower shower Put a shell under a drooping flower.

Diving board Lash five sticks together. Lash two long sticks to each side and push into the ground.

WATER RUN

With a water run you can collect your own rainwater, catch the drops and watch as they make a stream. Where will they go next?

COLLECT TOGETHER

From nature
- ☐ 2 sticks, both half an arm's-length
- ☐ A bunch of thick leaves of different sizes

From the Out Pack
- ☐ String
- ☐ Scissors
- ☐ Masking tape

HOW TO MAKE IT

1 Use an arm's-length of string to tie one end of the sticks together. Pull the other ends apart to make a 'v' shape.

2 Lay your leaves in a line on the ground, face down from biggest to smallest. Make sure each leaf overlaps the one before so there are no gaps.

3 Lay your 'v'-shaped sticks on top of your leaves, with the tied end at the same end as your smallest leaf.

4 Use masking tape to attach your sticks onto your leaves.

5 Turn it all over and then push the open sticks a little closer together. This will fold the leaves slightly to make a channel for your water to run down.

6 You can use your water run to fill up your fairy and elf pool (page 45). Put the tied end of the 'v' into the pool. Prop up the other end with sticks so the water will flow in. You could even place a few water runs around the pool to keep it as full as possible. Or perhaps you could put one underneath a drip coming from the roof of your house? The water run options are endless!

PRECIPITATION MOBILE

Can you remember how the water cycle works? With this precipitation mobile you'll never forget!

Sun: buttercups or yellow leaves tied with string

Clouds: cow parsley tied together with string

Rain: blue wool tied to the willow

Mountains: sticks tied onto the circle

Willow circle

Sea: oak leaves fixed on the back with masking tape

TROLL HOUSE

Down the stony path, past the leafy bushes and through the arching oak trees there's a happy stream giggling along. It flows gently under a little bridge, and it is just here that a grumpy little troll lives. His house is made of mud and stone, his door and window are made of the finest sticks and he has a sycamore leaf roof covered with luscious moss.

COLLECT TOGETHER

From nature
- [ ] Stones
- [ ] Leaves
- [ ] Moss
- [ ] 10 small sticks (each about a grown-up's finger-length)

From the Out Pack
- [ ] 1 wooden bead
- [ ] String
- [ ] Scissors
- [ ] Masking tape

HOW TO MAKE IT

1 To make the door, cut a piece of string of about two arm's-lengths.

2 Tie a fish-on-a-dish knot (clove hitch) onto the end of one of your sticks (see skills section, page 140).

3 Line up five sticks next to each other to make the door.

4 Lash the sticks to each other at one end of your door (see page 142), weaving your string under and over each stick in turn.

5 Tighten the string in between the sticks by winding the tail end of the string around each of the joints between the sticks.

6 Repeat steps 2–5 to lash together the other end of the door.

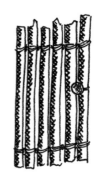

7 Thread the bead onto a small length of string. Attach this to one of the sticks where the troll's door handle should be. Tie a knot to secure.

8 To make the window, take three sticks and make a triangle shape, or take just one bendy stick and make a circle-shaped window. Fix them with tape.

9 Take two sticks and snap them into the right length to fit tight inside the window frame, and push them into place to make the windowpanes.

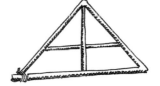

10 Prop up the door, and hook your window onto a stone, a stick or a small branch, or just push it into the mud. Now your troll can keep a look-out for goats.

How many Billy Goats Gruff
go trip-trapping over your bridge?
'Too many!' says the grumpy old troll!

This windiness we cannot see...

WIND

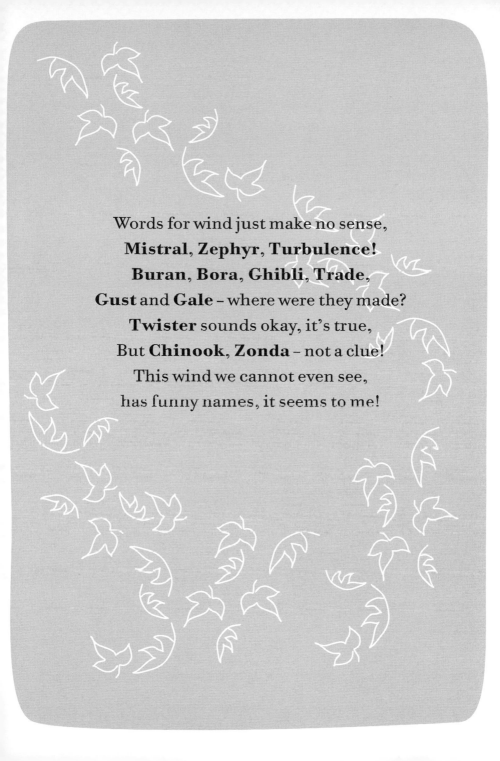

Words for wind just make no sense,
Mistral, Zephyr, Turbulence!
Buran, Bora, Ghibli, Trade,
Gust and **Gale** – where were they made?
Twister sounds okay, it's true,
But **Chinook, Zonda** – not a clue!
This wind we cannot even see,
has funny names, it seems to me!

TALKING ABOUT WIND

What a funny lot of words we use to describe this invisible thing that we call wind! Names that are not nearly as mean as the ones we use for rain. I think we must like wind more than rain! We might not be able to see wind, but we can definitely feel it, even the touch of the lightest breeze on our skin and through our hair. We can see the way it makes the grass twitch, the trees sway and the water ripple. At its most powerful, wind can lift cars into the air and knock trees to the ground – how can something we can't even see do such unbelievable things?

WIND IS AIR ON THE MOVE!

Air is all around us, everywhere. And that's especially good for us, because we need air all day long. We breathe it in and out, and it contains the oxygen our bodies need to survive. Yet we can't see it. So how do we know that it is there at all?

Try waving your hands in front of your face. Can you feel the cool of the air on your skin? Or perhaps blow onto your hand. Can you feel that? It is the air moving. And that is just the same as wind, except that wind is what happens when an enormous amount of air is on the move.

HOW DOES WIND HAPPEN?

Just like rain, it mainly has to do with the sun. The sun's heat warms up the air around us. When air gets warmer it gets bigger and lighter, and rises high up into the sky. And when air cools down it gets smaller and heavier, and sinks down to the ground. Wind happens when the cool air that is close to the ground moves into the areas left behind as the cold air rises.

There are some other things that help the air to create wind. One of them is the way in which our planet Earth spins on its axis. This has an effect on the wind that moves it around, and is called the Coriolis Effect (try to say that quickly!).

WONDERFUL WIND POWER

People have been using the power of wind for centuries. You can still see windmills from way back in time that were used for grinding flour or pumping water. You have probably seen big wind turbines with propeller blades that go round and round and round in the wind. The turbines turn the wind's power into electric energy that can be used to run all kinds of things, from electric cars to a toastie maker.

You may have played with pinwheels at the seaside. You can make your very own Out Pack pinwheel on page 84. Pinwheels have a similar design to the wind turbines all over the world that make energy from the wonderful power of the wind.

Electricity made from wind power is called renewable energy. Renewable energy comes from natural resources like waves, sunlight and wind that are not going to be used up. And as an added bonus, we can use them without doing a lot of messy damage to the planet.

PLAYING IN THE WIND

So what other amazing things can we do with wind? Humans are clever at making games and sports out of almost anything, and wind is no exception. Here are just a few games that use the wind: sailing, wind surfing, kiting (make your own on page 77) kite surfing, gliding, hang-gliding (make your own on page 94), paragliding, paramotoring, microlighting and land surfing. That's quite a list, but there are probably even more!

MEASURING THE GUSTS AND GALES

I wonder if you've ever noticed that sometimes there is hardly any wind at all? The trees don't move, and the surface of the river is like a mirror. And yet on other days it feels like wind is going to sweep you clean off your feet! Just like the difference between a mizzly drizzle and a downpour when it's raining, wind can be very gentle and also super-strong.

People have been measuring the wind for centuries. Probably the most widely known measurement for wind is the Beaufort scale. It was created by a man called Sir Francis Beaufort and is a lovely way to describe how blowy it is on a certain day.

The Beaufort scale goes from 0 to 12, with 0 very calm and still and 12 being one of the strongest winds in the world.

OUR BEAUFORT SCALE

0 Not a breath of wind. Everything is still, like a statue.

1 All the leaves are still, but if you spot smoke coming out of a chimney or bonfire, it will be moving a little.

2 The leaves next to your wellies are twitching.

3 The leaves next to your wellies are now tickling your wellies.

4 Your hair is getting swished about and small tree branches are starting to sway.

5 Small trees are moving, as if they're giving you a wave.

6 Your brolly has blown inside out or the empty bin has fallen over!

7 All sorts of trees are being blown to and fro. And it's so windy that it's a bit hard to walk.

8 Twigs and branches are flying off the trees. Even cars are getting pushed about. Time to watch from indoors!

9 The poor old trees are getting blown about. And look, there goes a road sign!

10 It's really stormy now; I hope everyone's inside. Big trees might topple over and tiles fall off the roof.

11 It's super-stormy now. Trees and houses are really getting it.

12 I hope you've battened down your hatches. This really is as stormy as you could possibly imagine! The wind is picking up everything in its path and hurling it about. This is the super-est mega-power wind.

WHERE IS IT COMING FROM?

Hoist the sails me hearties, because there be a northwesterly coming in! When the weather people (or pirates!) talk about wind direction, they are talking about where it is coming from. So a northwesterly is a wind that's coming from the north-west.

Stand outside with your own weather vane (page 80) and ask your mum or dad to point out where North is. Stand looking in that direction and see which way the wind blows your weather vane. The arrow will point to where the wind is coming from.

Use the clever way of finding out exactly which direction the wind is coming from with wind stones (page 82).

Knowing what the wind is doing is very important for some people. The weather people need to know where the wind is blowing the clouds to and how fast. Then they can tell us when to expect rain or storms. People flying planes or sailing on the sea need to know what the weather's doing, to stay safe and to use the wind to help their journeys. Even drivers of big lorries need to know if it's too windy to go on the road.

GOING OUT IN THE WIND

Here is our checklist for having a quick adventure, whatever the wind is doing today!

- **Feel the wind.** Is it gentle or pushy, blustery or howling? Is it gusty, starty and stoppy, or does it just keep on blowing?

- **Listen.** Does it sound swishy and whistling, or bangy and booming?

- **What can you smell?** Flowers, or smoke, or maybe cow poo!

- We can't see the wind, but can see what it does. **What's being blown about?** Trees, bushes, flowers, clouds, hats, clothes, brollies…what else is on the move?

- You can't really taste wind either, but you can feel it on your tongue. Stick it out and try!

- **Where's the wind coming from?** Can you find something that will float in the breeze? Leaves, catkins, winged seeds? Throw them up in the air and see where they land.

- **Who gets the swishy hair prize?**

WIND QUICKIES

Just like with rain, we want you to get out and enjoy the wind as soon as it arrives. When the wind is really blowing outside, you might not have lots of time for making things. Here are a few quick wind activities. You can pop outside and play for a short time and then pop back inside again!

CLOUD RACING

Lie on the grass and watch the clouds float by. There are all shapes and sizes, types and speeds. Choose one – is it the fastest? Watch it and see.

WIND TARGETS

Outdoor sports people will tell you how much the wind changes the way they play their games. See for yourself. Make a target on the ground using sticks and stones. Gather your wonderful finds: grass, leaves, catkins, a winged seed. Can you guess what the wind will do when you try to throw them at your target? Which ones work best?

LEAF CHASING

In autumn, when the trees are losing their leaves and some drop winged seeds, it's a lot of fun to chase about trying to catch them. Ask a mum or dad or a grown-up who's with you to time you and your friends to see who can catch the most in a minute.

Or you can pick up huge piles that have fallen from the trees. They're so much fun to pick up and throw into the breeze. Watch how far they fly.

DANDELION CLOCKS

Have you ever blown a dandelion clock? If it's between late spring and autumn, hunt for one and give it a try. They are called clocks because you have to count the number of puffs it takes to blow all the seeds away – that's supposed to be the time in Dandelion-time! If it's windy you can blow the seeds up into the air and watch them dance in the breeze.

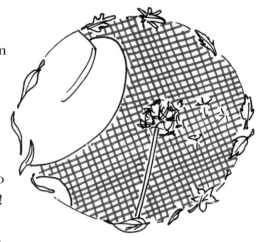

WIND ART

Watch as the wind brings your art to life! Try making a dragon that breathes roaring flames or a puppet with dancing legs. Attach leaves or other light nature treasures to wool so they can flutter in the breeze. Weigh them down with other parts of your picture, such as heavy stones, rocks and branches. 3-D moving art – no glasses required!

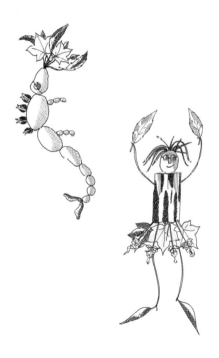

WIND SPINNER

A windy day is the perfect day to make a wind spinner!

COLLECT TOGETHER

From nature
- [ ] About 25 thin sticks, about a grown-up's hand-length long

From the Out Pack
- [ ] Garden wire
- [ ] Wool
- [ ] Scissors
- [ ] Beads

HOW TO MAKE IT

1 Take one stick and an arm's-length of garden wire. Attach one end of the wire to the middle of the stick with a pinch and twist.

2 Place another stick next to this one and wind the garden wire around it, then between the two sticks and back around the first one. Now bring the wire back in between the two sticks. Try to keep the wire quite tight so that the sticks stay close together.

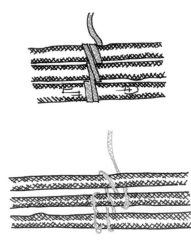

3 Take another stick and place it next to the second stick. Wrap the garden wire around this stick and back around the second stick in the same way, always feeding the wire in and out of the sticks.

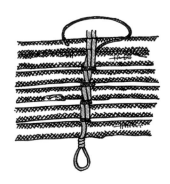

4 Keep doing this until all the sticks are attached to each other with garden wire.

5 With the remaining wire at the top, make a loop to hang your spinner, with a pinch and twist.

6 Take an arm's-length of wool and tie it to the top stick on your wind spinner.

7 This wool is to go round each of the wire joins that connect the sticks. Wind your wool all the way around the wire join, pulling it tight. Then move onto the next join, all the way around and pull tight. On the back of the spinner this will give you a 'z' pattern. Your wool should go all the way down the spine of your spinner, tightening and strengthening it.

8 Attach a few beads to the ends of the wool at the bottom of the spinner.

9 Finally, from the top of your spinner make a twist, spreading out each stick about a finger apart all the way down.

10 With a piece of wool, hang your spinner somewhere outside, on your house or on a tree...anywhere it can catch the wind. Watch it twirl and dance.

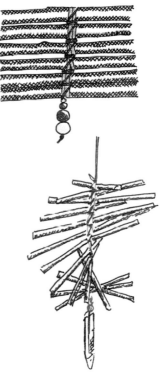

WIND SOCK

Airports hang up special wind socks to see the direction of the wind and how strong it is. Not quite the same as your smelly socks! Our grass wind sock is perfect for the fairy and elf airport.

COLLECT TOGETHER

From nature
- [ ] Long and thick blades of grass or thin leaves
- [ ] 1 arm's-length stick

From the Out Pack
- [ ] Masking tape
- [ ] Scissors
- [ ] Paperclip
- [ ] String

HOW TO MAKE IT

1 Cut half an arm's-length of masking tape and lay it flat on the ground, sticky side up. This is quite tricky because the tape sticks to your hands. Try using your stick or two stones to keep the ends down.

2 Lay another piece of masking tape on the ground, parallel to your first piece. The space in between should be a little shorter than the length of your grass.

3 Lay your blades of grass one after the other, from one piece of tape to the other, starting at the bottom of the masking tape. It doesn't matter if there are small gaps between the blades. Do this until you are halfway along the tape.

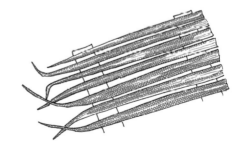

4 Now fold the remaining tape back over the top of the blades of grass, like a grass sandwich. Leave a little bit of tape hanging over to stick your sock together.

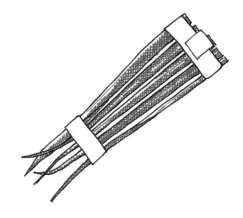

5 Roll both pieces of masking tape over to make a funnel shape that's wider at one end. Secure this with the extra masking tape you left at the end.

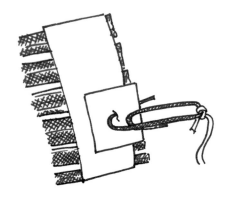

6 Stick an extra bit of masking tape on the wider end of the funnel and thread the end of a paperclip through it.

7 Tie or stick one end of a hand's-length of string to the paperclip and the other end to the stick.

8 Push the stick into some soft ground where your wind sock is likely to catch the breeze.

9 Now you can tell when it's safe for fairy and elf pilots to fly. Come on, pull your socks up!

KITE

Run into the wind and your woven grass kite will fly.
Dance and dart, and catch the eye of passers-by...

COLLECT TOGETHER

From nature
- [ ] 2 thin, hand-length sticks
- [ ] A good handful of thick grass or thin leaves
- [ ] A handful of small leaves

From the Out Pack
- [ ] Masking tape
- [ ] Scissors
- [ ] String
- [ ] Wool

HOW TO MAKE IT

The first part of making the kite is like the wind sock, except that for the kite we will be weaving the grass. You can learn a bit more about how to weave in the skills section, page 144. Or you can just follow these directions.

1 Cut half an arm's-length of masking tape and lay it flat on the ground, sticky side up. It is quite tricky because the tape sticks to your hands. Use your stick or two stones to keep the ends down.

2 Lay another piece of masking tape on the ground, parallel to your first piece. The space in between should be a little shorter than the length of your grass.

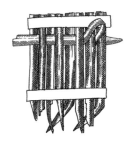

3 Lay your blades of grass from one piece of tape to the other in a row. For this one, it's better if the blades of grass are right next to each other with no gaps.

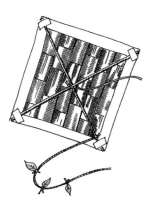

4 Now lay another piece of masking tape over the top of each of the first pieces of masking tape, this time sticky side down, to secure the grass.

5 You are now going to weave. Take a new blade of grass and weave it under and then over your taped grass, until you reach the end.

6 Do this again, but this time start with an over then under. Continue this alternating pattern until you reach the other end.

7 Stick the loose ends of grass down with masking tape. You should now have nice woven grasses.

8 Put your two sticks in a cross shape and tie them together with one end of two-arm's-lengths of string.

9 To make your kite's tail, first make some bows. For each bow stick two small leaves together with masking tape. Now tie the wool around the middle of each pair of leaves

to make a string of bows, spaced out along the tail. Tie one end of the wool to the end of one of your sticks.

10 Attach the ends of the sticks to each corner of your grass square with finger-lengths of masking tape.

11 Now grab your kite by its string, run into the wind and watch it fly.

WEATHER VANE

Where is that wind coming from? From north or south, from east or west? Your weather vane will help you to find out.

COLLECT TOGETHER

From nature
- [ ] 1 half-arm's-length stick
- [ ] 1 hand-length stick
- [ ] 2 short sticks
- [ ] A big leaf

From the Out Pack
- [ ] 1 bead
- [ ] Masking tape
- [ ] Scissors
- [ ] Garden wire
- [ ] String
- [ ] Pens

HOW TO MAKE IT

1 Secure a bead to one end of the long stick with masking tape. The hole in the bead needs to be facing upwards and you should be able to see through it.

2 Cut a hand's-length of garden wire and then twist it around the middle of the hand-length stick. Secure it with a pinch and twist. This should fit into your bead.

3 To make the pointy tip of your arrow, lash (see skills section, page 142) the two small sticks into a 'v' shape leaving two ends of excess string. Use the excess string to tie it to one end of the hand-length stick to be the tail of your arrow.

4 Then cut a 'v' shape into the top of a leaf and secure it to the other end of your hand-length stick with masking tape.

5 Hold the hand-length stick by the twisted garden wire and move the wire along until the stick is balanced. Secure the loop of the wire to the hand-length stick with a very small piece of masking tape.

6 Thread the wire into the bead so the arrow is balancing. Now hold your weather vane by the long stick and blow on the arrow to test it.

WIND STONES

Which direction is the wind coming from, can you tell?
Mark four stones with N, S, E and W (North, South, East and
West). Take two sticks of about the same length. Ask your mum
or dad, or grown-up with you, which way north is and put one
stick down pointing towards the North. Place your N stone at the
top and your S stone at the bottom. Now put your other stick over
your first one to make a cross. Place your E stone on the right and
your W stone on the left.

WEATHER VANE GAME

Here's a good game that's fun to play with others on a gusty day. Stand still and hold the weather vane. Everyone else decides to try and get from one side of the garden to the other, or it could be from one side of the playground to a very big tree. It's up to you.

The only rule is that everyone has to move in the direction that the weather vane is pointing. Every time the wind direction changes your weather vane will move, then everyone has to move in the new direction. It can be very funny! See who gets to the other side first.

PINWHEEL

Here's how to make a pinwheel out of leaves.

COLLECT TOGETHER

From nature
- [ ] 4 narrow, waxy leaves
- [ ] 1 stick

From the Out Pack
- [ ] 9 paperclips
- [ ] Masking tape
- [ ] Garden wire
- [ ] Scissors
- [ ] 4 beads

HOW TO MAKE IT

1 Curl each of your leaves into a cone and secure with two paperclips.

2 Take two of your curled leaf cones and fix them together with masking tape over the paperclips. Do the same with the other pair and make sure the paperclips all cross each other.

3 Unfold another paperclip and use it to pierce a hole through the crossed paperclips and masking tape.

4 Take half an arm's-length of wire and thread it through the hole.

5 Bring the wire around to the back of the pinwheel and pinch and twist. Keep twisting until you have twisted nearly all of the garden wire.

6 Secure the middle of the pinwheel with a few layers of masking tape.

7 Take the twisted garden wire and thread the ends through two beads.

8 For your pinwheel stick, attach a bead with four thin finger-lengths of masking tape on the very top of the stick. The bead should be nearly horizontal but the hole should be angled slightly upwards. This is to stop your pinwheel hitting your stick as it turns.

9 Thread the twisted garden wire through this bead.

10 Take one final bead and thread this on the wire behind the stick. Make a knot with the remaining garden wire as tight as you can but make sure the pinwheel can still move.

11 Now – blow! And watch your pinwheel go round.

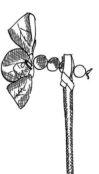

WIND CHIMES

Find things from nature that make a sound when they hit against each other. Add them to your wind chime. Perhaps a stick wind chime, a stone or a pine cone one, or a mixture. Now listen out for a gusty breeze.

This activity starts with the season star, a favourite from our first book, *Let's Go Outside*. If you only want to make a season star, just do steps 1 to 5. If you would like a wind chime for your garden, keep going!

COLLECT TOGETHER

From nature
- [ ] 5 hand-length sticks for star
- [ ] 5 longer sticks for chimes (or 5 other finds to hang as chimes)

From the Out Pack
- [ ] 10 elastic bands
- [ ] 5 paperclips
- [ ] Wool
- [ ] Scissors
- [ ] String

HOW TO MAKE IT

1 To make a star shape, take your five hand-length sticks and fix them together with elastic bands at alternate ends, so that they form a zig-zag.

2 Place them on the floor in a zig-zag so that the start of the zig-zag looks like a 'w'.

3 Take stick 1 and cross it over stick 3 to make your first star point.

4 Take stick 4 and cross it over sticks 1 and 2.

5 Take stick 5 behind the top point to complete your star. Fix sticks 1 and 5 together with an elastic band to make the final point.

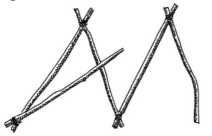

6 To make your chimes, fix a paperclip to the top of each chime stick using an elastic band. Tie two hand-lengths of wool to each paperclip.

7 Tie a chime to each point of your star using this wool. Wrap the wool around each star point and tie off so the chimes hang down at the same height and can hit each other to make a sound.

8 Wrap a hand-length of wool around the centre of the star and hang the last chime from the middle.

9 Tie two hand-lengths of string from the middle of the star so it will balance.

10 You can decorate your chimes by wrapping wool or string around them.

FAIRY AND ELF WASHING LINE

Where else would garden fairies and elves hang their washing out to dry?

Elf shirt: large leaf, cut to shape

Fairy day skirt: sycamore seeds fastened with masking tape

Elf trousers: two leaves, cut to shape

Fairy party skirt: grasses and wild flowers fastened with masking tape and decorated with felt-tip pen.

FRISBEES

A hoop of willow + a handful of leaves = Frisbee...who knew?!

COLLECT TOGETHER

From nature
- [ ] 2 long shoots of willow, snapped at their joins.
- [ ] A handful of leaves

From the Out Pack
- [ ] Wool
- [ ] Scissors

HOW TO MAKE IT

1 Make a circle with one end of your willow shoot.

2 Feed the other end of the shoot in and out of your circle, round and round until there is no willow left. This is your willow hoop.

3 Take the second willow shoot and feed it in and out of your willow hoop to add strength. Tuck the end into the hoop.

4 Take a three-arm's-length of wool and tie the end onto one side of your hoop. Wind the wool from one side of the hoop to another, moving round until there is wool criss-crossed all over the hoop. Tie the other end of the wool to the hoop to fix it.

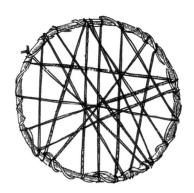

5 Stuff your leaves into the middle of your wool mesh.

6 Now you have a leafy Frisbee. Give it a throw and see it fly.

ZIPLINE HANG-GLIDER

This little hang-glider pilot is off to coast on the thermals!

COLLECT TOGETHER

From nature

- [ ] 2 hand-length sticks and 1 two-hand-length stick
- [ ] 3 half-hand-length sticks
- [ ] 1 short, thin stick
- [ ] A pinch of grass
- [ ] 5 or 6 thick waxy leaves

From the Out Pack

- [ ] String
- [ ] Scissors
- [ ] Masking tape
- [ ] Paperclip
- [ ] 1 elastic band
- [ ] 1 small bead and 4 bigger beads
- [ ] Garden wire

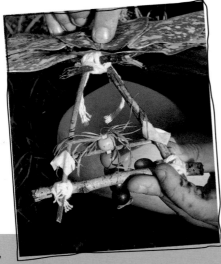

HOW TO MAKE IT

1 Lash (see skills section, page 142) the three bigger sticks into a triangle shape to make the wing.

2 Fan out your leaves to the size of your triangle and place them face down. Put your triangle on top of them. Secure the triangle to the leaves with masking tape.

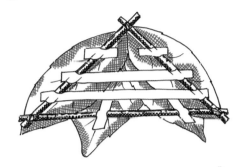

3 Lash your three half-hand-length sticks into a triangle to make your crossbar. The join at the point of the triangle you're going to use as your top point should be as close to the top of the sticks as possible.

4 Take a piece of string two hand-lengths long and tie the middle of it to the top point of the little triangle.

5 Tie these ends to either side of the bigger triangle (about halfway down each side). Make sure that it's quite taut so that the little triangle hangs just below the leaves.

6 To make your zipwire loop, fold a hand-length of string in half and knot the midpoint to one end of your paperclip. Now wrap a finger-length of masking tape around the string and the paperclip, leaving the top loop of the paperclip uncovered.

7 Make a hole in the middle of the wing, directly above the top join of the little triangle. Thread the ends of the string attached to the paperclip through the hole and tie a granny knot (see skills section, page 143) onto the top join of the little triangle.

8 To make your hang-glider pilot, flatten your elastic band and thread it through your little bead to make the pilot's head. Push the bead near to the end of the elastic band, leaving just a small loop of elastic band to thread the grass through. This is your pilot's hair!

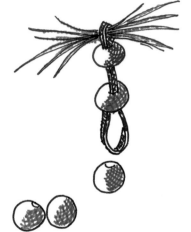

9 Thread three more beads onto the elastic band.

10 Take a finger-length of garden wire and secure one end to the loose loop at the bottom of the elastic band, with a pinch and twist.

11 Thread the wire through your last bead, pulling it tight. Pinch, twist and fold the wire and this should pull the grass hair tight on your pilot's head.

12 For your pilot's arms, take your short, thin stick and push it through the elastic band between your first bead (the pilot's head) and the others (the pilot's body).

13 Secure the pilot's arms to the crossbar with a small amount of masking tape. Make sure the pilot is pointing forwards!

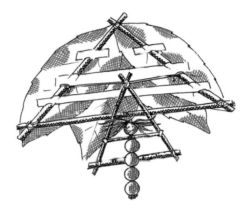

14 Thread the paperclip loop onto a length of string or garden wire. Suspend the string between two points to create a zipwire. If the breeze is gentle you can make one end of the zipwire lower so that gravity gives a helping hand.

Check the wing, take the crossbar, look to the horizon and run. Lift off!

FLUTTERBY

Watch as your leafy butterfly flutters in the breeze.

COLLECT TOGETHER

From nature
- [ ] 4 waxy leaves

From the Out Pack
- [ ] Paperclip
- [ ] Masking tape
- [ ] Scissors
- [ ] Garden wire
- [ ] 5 small beads and 1 big bead
- [ ] String
- [ ] Pen

HOW TO MAKE IT

1 Attach two of your leaves to your paperclip with masking tape. Make sure the leaves are crossed to make the flutterby's lower wings.

2 Take the other two leaves and attach them by their stems with masking tape to make the upper wings.

3 Attach the upper wings to the lower wings using a short piece of masking tape.

4 To make the body of the butterfly, take two hand-lengths of garden wire. Thread three of the smaller beads onto the wire until they are halfway along.

5 Fold the wire back over the three smaller beads and secure with a pinch and twist.

6 Thread the twisted ends of wire through the bigger head bead and tie a granny knot (see skills section, page 143) in the wire to secure it.

7 To make your flutterby's antennae, tie a small bead to each of the two ends of wire.

8 Draw a face on the head bead.

9 Take a hand-length of garden wire and tie the middle of it to the flutterby's body and the leaf wings. Secure the wire with a pinch and twist.

10 Attach your flutterby to a short piece of string, so you can hold on as it flutters in the breeze.

DAMSELS AND DRAGONS

Do you know the difference between a dragonfly and a damselfly? You have probably seen them hovering over streams or ponds.

Here's a rhyme to help:

Dragonfly wings two **big** two **small**
Damselfly wings **the same** all four
Dragonfly rests with **wings out wide**
Damselfly folds them **to the sides**

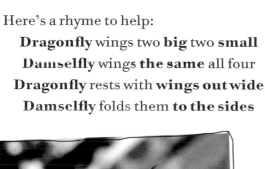

COLLECT TOGETHER

From nature
- ☐ 4 leaves (4 the same for damselflies and 2 thin and 2 thick for dragonflies)
- ☐ 1 bendy stick that is thin enough to thread beads on

From the Out Pack
- ☐ Masking tape
- ☐ Scissors
- ☐ Garden wire
- ☐ 8 beads of different sizes
- ☐ 2 elastic bands
- ☐ Pen

HOW TO MAKE IT

1 Take two matching leaves and fix them together with masking tape to make a pair of wings. Do the same for the other two leaves.

2 Cut a hand-length of garden wire, fold it in half around the two sets of leaves and attach it all together with a pinch and twist.

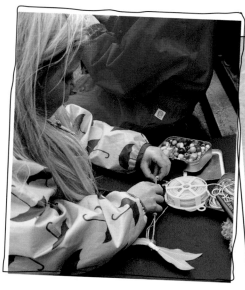

3 Thread the two loose ends of wire through a big bead and secure the wire with a pinch and twist. The loose ends of wire become two legs.

4 Cut two finger-lengths of garden wire and thread them through the wire. Secure them with a pinch and twist. This will make your insect's other legs.

5 Wrap an elastic band around your stick, roughly halfway down. This acts as a stopper for your beads. Make the abdomen of your insect by threading the small beads onto the stick.

6 Thread a big bead onto the stick and then the winged bead to make the body.

7 Thread a final big bead onto the stick and draw two eyes on it. A dragonfly's eyes are usually close together.

A damselfly's eyes are further apart.

8 Secure all of the beads onto your stick using an elastic band.

9 Now watch them fly into the sky...damsels and dragons way up high.

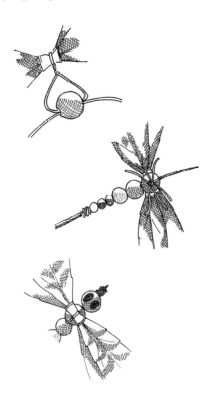

SNOW

'To appreciate the beauty of a snowflake,
it's necessary to stand out in the cold.'
Unknown

No one but the **Inuit**
Knows more about the snow
They **live and work** and play on it,
The snow is how they **flow**
So when they talk of white stuff
Their words don't go to waste
They've names for **every kind** of snow,
Perhaps you'd like a **taste**!

INUIT WORDS FOR SNOW

The Inuits are thought to have about 50 words for snow. Here are just six of our favourites.

Tlapa
Powder snow. The freshly fallen stuff.

Blotla
Blowing snow. When a gust whips the snow up round your face.

Mactla
Snow burgers! With freezing cold fries please!

Shlim
Slush! When snow is melting but isn't quite water.

Pritla
Our children's snow. Imagine having snow just for you!

Naklin
Forgotten snow. Perhaps the Inuit have so much snow that they forget about some of it!

SNOW!

Isn't it just the best? The excitement that comes with the arrival of those first few flakes of snow falling gently from the sky is virtually indescribable. It means so many things that we love. Hot chocolate, sledges, snowballs, carrot noses, icicles – and sometimes a whole day off school. Who could possibly not love snow?

WINTER WEATHER

Snow comes in wintertime, the coldest season of the year. As we move through autumn and into winter, day by day the sun sets earlier and rises later. It is dark quite a lot of the time. The days get colder, and eventually there are signs that the world around us is freezing. Even if it is not a billowing snowstorm, there may be gentle touches of frost on grass and car windows, or perhaps a puddle frozen over with ice. Perhaps snow is on the way. But watch out for that icy weather. It might look beautiful but you could slip and fall on your bum!

HOW IS SNOW MADE?

Do you remember the water cycle, from our chapter on rain? Up in the sky, water vapour from the seas and oceans is changing back into water droplets. It's how the clouds are made and it's called condensation. The difference with snow is that this time it's *really* cold up there. As the water vapour condenses back into water, instead of the teeny-tiny water droplets that come together to make rain, tiny ice crystals are formed. More and more ice crystals stick together to make snowflakes, all in a completely tiny and exceptionally beautiful way. It's nice to think that each delicate and unique snowflake is actually a few ice crystals having a hug!

In the clouds, snowflakes hug each other too, and when they are heavy enough they fall to the ground. If the ground is cold enough and enough snowflakes fall, they stick to the ground and more and more of them pile on top. Before you know it, the whole world around you has turned white. Everything is calm and beautiful. The air is fresh and crisp. The ground under your feet crunches. Pure magic!

DON'T FORGET HAIL!

Snow only happens in winter weather, but hailstorms can happen at any time of year. Just like rain and snow, water vapour rises up in the air until it meets much cooler air. But this time the vapour is sucked high up into big cumulonimbus thunderclouds that are already cold and icy on top. The vapour turns into balls or pieces of ice called hailstones. When they are too heavy to stay in the cloud, they start to fall.

Watch the hailstones bounce on the ground or on the cars and even on your head. Hailstones can be pea-sized, marble-sized, golf ball-sized and even tennis ball-sized. Even the size of a grapefruit! But usually they are not that big. If the hail is teeny-tiny, maybe you can catch a hailstone in your hand and watch it melt – like magic.

'Goodbye thundercloud' said the hail,
as down to earth he sped
Steering, veering, right on course
to bash you on the head!

SNOWY SPORTS AND GAMES

There is all kinds of fun to be had on the snow and ice, especially on mountains with snowy slopes. There's skiing, when you wear special long planks on your feet to help you slide downhill, and other sports like snowboarding, snow blading, bobsleighing and ski jumping. On the ice there is speed skating, figure skating, ice hockey and curling.

There are some special kinds of sledging with funny names, called luge and skeleton. Perhaps you've been on a sledge (and you can make a fairy sledge on page 132). And don't forget all those snowy games like building snowmen, making snow angels and having snowball fights.

GOING OUT ON A SNOWY DAY

❄ Listen to the sound snow makes. It crunches under your feet. But the snow can change the world around us. Can you hear how quiet it all sounds?

❄ Look around at how the snow covers everything. A bit like a blanket. What does it look like to you?

❄ Taste it. Stick out your tongue to catch a snowflake. Or ask mum or dad to pick some clean snow for you to taste.

❄ Smell it. Does the world smell different? Or perhaps it makes your nose all cold inside.

❄ Feel it. On your face, on your hands. So crisp and refreshing.

STAYING WARM IN THE SNOW

Snow is lovely to touch but can also make you very cold. The trick to enjoying snow is keeping warm and dry, then you can play for hours. So put on your warmest of warm clothes and take a hot drink.

- Layers of T-shirts and jumpers and a thick waterproof coat.

- Thick waterproof trousers if you have them, or thin ones with some warm trousers underneath will be just as snuggly.

- A warm hat, a scarf and some warm waterproof gloves. Ski gloves are good.

- Some lovely thick socks to go inside your wellies, or a few pairs of thin ones.

- Ask your mum or dad if they can bring a flask of hot chocolate to drink.

- Last of all, make sure your parents have their warmest clothes on too. Sometimes grown-ups are so busy getting the children properly dressed that they forget about themselves and end up having a miserable time. Look after them!

SNOW QUICKIES

Everyone grab your warmest clothes, your hat, scarf, gloves and boots. Now run outside and have fun with these quick activities.

DINO PRINTS

Any footprints are fun to make in snow. Small ones, great big stompy ones, daddy ones, mummy ones and even little baby ones. You could make a maze of footprints or a trail for your friends to follow. Where does it lead? Or how about the pre-historic tracks of a tyrannosaurus rex? Or even a brachiosaurus? Do you dare to follow those?

TREE SNOWSTORM

Find yourself a wibbly-wobbly tree and give it a gentle shake. Did you get covered in snow? Ask a friend or mum or dad to come under the tree to look at something amazing...then shake! TREE SNOWSTORM!

SNOW ANGEL

People have been enjoying making these for years. To make
your snow angel, lie down on the snow with your arms by your
sides and your legs together. Then swish your arms up above
your head, keeping them in the snow, and then back down and
up again. This makes your angel's wings. And swish your legs as
wide as possible and back together again as well. This will make
your angel's flowing gown. Carefully stand up and admire your
beautiful creation!

SLEDGING

If you live near a gentle hill that hasn't got fences or hedges in the way, you can have fun sledging. You'll need to bring a sledge. You can buy all kinds, from little plastic ones to big wooden toboggans.

SNOWMEN

Why just snowMEN? Why not snow women, snow monsters, snow dragons or snow fairies? Let your imagination go wild. Let's build all kinds of wonderful snowy creatures.

ANIMAL FOOTPRINTS

Tracking animal footprints in the snow is enormous fun. Look hard and you're sure to find some. Here are our favourites.

Dogs! You can spot doggy pawprints easily. They have four toes, with claws that you might be able to see. They have a small heel pad just behind their toes. Why not find a dog and follow its footprints in the snow?

Cats! You might be lucky enough to see a cat prowling through the snow. Cat pawprints are similar to dogs' prints but they are smaller and rounder. They have four toes but a bigger heel pad, and you probably won't be able to see their claw prints.

Rabbits! These might be a little harder to come by but they are easy to spot. There will usually be two little front legs behind two bigger back legs, followed by a big gap before the next ones as the rabbit bounds through the air. All the prints tend to be an oval shape.

Squirrels! A little bit like rabbit prints, but different because squirrels have long, thin toes. When squirrels are running fast they bring their back legs around the outside of their front legs and bound away with all their might. So you will see a little cluster of four footprints. An amazing thing is that the back leg prints, on the outside, have five toes and the front legs, on the inside, have four. These are a great print to find.

Birds! There are many different types of bird prints, but nearly all birds have super-thin claws. The prints look a little bit as if they were made with a very tiny twig. Perhaps you can find a twig and make some more...

MR SNOWMAN HEAD

Do you want to build a snowman? Or perhaps just build his head! For this extremely fun activity you can create your accessories anytime, so you are ready to make this Mr Snowman Head as crazy as you like, as soon as the snow settles on the ground.

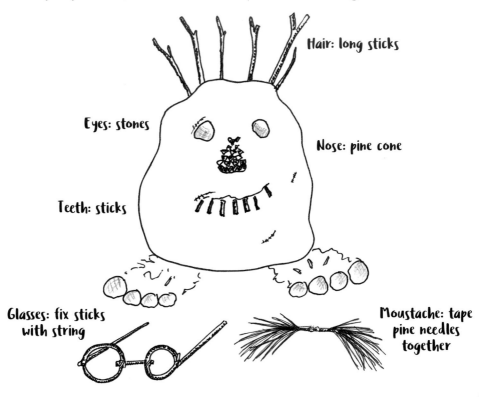

Hair: long sticks

Eyes: stones

Nose: pine cone

Teeth: sticks

Glasses: fix sticks with string

Moustache: tape pine needles together

SNOWBALL FORT

Stockpile your snowballs ready for the big showdown! Your snowballs also make part of the fort you can build to hide behind. It can have walls, a doorway, even turrets and as many knights as you can imagine! Then, on your marks, go – time to have a snowball fight. Just take your snowballs straight off your fort!

YETI FEET

Hair: roughen the snow with a stick
then add pine needles and sticks

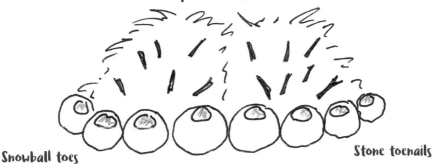

Snowball toes

Stone toenails

Yetis are supposed to be big furry creatures a bit like apes that live in the snowy Himalayan mountains, but nobody knows if they really exist. Another name for a Yeti is an Abominable Snowman – try saying that one quickly a few times! Imagine having enormous Yeti feet, huge and fluffy with great big toes. Stomp about and get abominable in the snow!

SNOW NOUGHTS AND CROSSES

Are you tired out from making snowmen and having snowball fights? Here's a calm game in the snow. Some might know it as tic-tac-toe.

Find some nice long sticks, between an arm's-length and two arm's-lengths. Place them on the ground in a grid.

How to play One player is crosses and the other is noughts. Players can draw noughts and crosses in the snow with a stick, or even use snowballs for the noughts. The youngest player goes first.

The aim of the game The winner is the first person to get either three noughts or three crosses in a line, across the board, from top to bottom, or from one corner to the opposite one, diagonally. The first player puts either their nought or cross in one of the spaces, then the other player does the same in another space. Take turns until one of the players has got three of their noughts or crosses in a line, or until there are no spaces left.

Another go? Just rub out your noughts and crosses or move your sticks somewhere else. Tic-Tac-Toe in the snow!

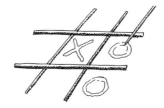

SNOW GOLF

Snow golf is played in the snow with flags and holes rather than on grass. It's for any age and any number of players. It's cold, so this is a short golf course with only four holes! The aim is to be the first person to have got your ball into all the holes in the fewest hits.

COLLECT TOGETHER

From nature
- [ ] Lots of pine needles or furry pine leaves or teeny-tiny pine cones. Anything that's not frozen or snowy, to make a ball.
- [ ] 11 leaves, 10 small and 1 big
- [ ] 4 sticks about half an arm's-length

From the Out Pack
- [ ] Masking tape
- [ ] Scissors
- [ ] Felt-tip pens

MAKE YOUR GOLF EQUIPMENT

Make an evergreen ball for each player from your nature finds. Wrap them all up in masking tape, round and round until all your evergreen is hidden.

You can decorate the balls with your felt-tip pens.

SET UP YOUR GOLF COURSE

First make your flags. Attach one leaf to a stick with masking tape. Then attach two leaves to a stick for the next flag, then make flags with three leaves and four leaves in the same way.

Dig four holes in the snow that are big enough for your evergreen balls to roll into. Push a flag in to the ground beside each hole. Put a big starting leaf on the ground at the beginning of the course.

HOW TO PLAY

The youngest player goes first. Each player, in turn, places their ball on the starting leaf and hits it towards the first hole. They should count how many hits it takes them to get their ball in the hole. The next player does the same and this continues for all holes.

The winner is the player who hit their ball into all holes in the fewest hits.

More or less of a challenge
Young children could have a free hit per turn. To make it more challenging, make the course longer, or put in obstacles. If you like, you can make crazy golf paths and ramps and wiggles with sticks and pine cones, or anything else you find.

BIRD AND SQUIRREL PLATES

Have you still got any of your autumn foragings? Conkers, beech nuts, acorns, sweet chestnuts or sunflower seeds? If so, then you can arrange a dinner plate for the birds and squirrels. It's hard for animals to find food in the wintertime, especially when the ground is covered in snow or ice. Make them a special dinner treat.

SNOW QUEEN PALACE

An icy puddle is all you need to construct a frozen palace for the snow queen. Make sure you're wearing nice thick gloves and watch out for sharp edges. Carefully lift the shards of ice and balance them against one another. Can you draw a window or door on the ice with the end of a paperclip?

Carefully scratch windows into the ice with a paperclip. Rest the ice shards against a stone or small stump

Door: lash together small sticks. Add a bead with garden wire

FAIRY SLEDGE

If you were a fairy then we could make you a sledge using only the Out Pack and nature. Are you a fairy? No? What a shame! Let's make a sledge for your garden fairies then – they are going to love it!

COLLECT TOGETHER

From nature

☐ 5 hand-length sticks

☐ 4 finger-length sticks

☐ 2 one-and-a-half hand-length, slightly bent sticks

From the Out Pack

☐ String

☐ Scissors

HOW TO MAKE IT

1 Cut a piece of string of about two arms'-lengths.

2 Tie a fish-on-a-dish knot (clove hitch) onto the end of one of your hand-length sticks (see skills section, page 140).

3 Take all of your hand-length sticks and line them up next to each other.

4 Lash (see skills section, page 142) the sticks together by weaving your string under and over each of the sticks in turn.

5 Tighten the string in between the sticks by winding the tail-end of the string around each of the four joints.

6 Repeat steps 2–5 at the other end of the sledge.

7 Attach your finger-length sticks with elastic bands to each corner of the sledge, so it looks a bit like a table.

8 Now attach the runners to your sledge. Cut your masking tape into strips. Take your slightly bent sticks and attach them to the finger-length sticks with the masking tape.

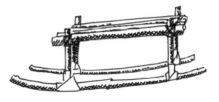

9 Now the fairies can get on board and have a mad sledge ride down the hill.

FROST FLAKES

This activity is a bit of a science experiment. Make your very own frost flake, decorated with bits and pieces from nature. Wait for a very cold and frosty night then hang it outdoors, throw some water over it and wait until the morning. Have you managed to make your very own frost? Marvel at the beautiful shards of frost that have grown on your very own frost flake.

COLLECT TOGETHER

From nature
- [ ] 4 short sticks, 4 longer sticks and 2 arm-length sticks
- [ ] Feathers
- [ ] Nuts
- [ ] Pine cones
- [ ] Leaves

From the Out Pack
- [ ] String
- [ ] Scissors
- [ ] Masking tape
- [ ] Wool

HOW TO MAKE IT

1 Firstly, to make your frost flake, lash (see skills section, page 140) the two longest sticks together in a cross with string.

2 Take four of the bigger of your shorter sticks and lash them onto the four ends of the longer sticks.

3 Take four short sticks and lash these wherever you like in other places on the centre cross. Is this looking more and more like a frost flake?

4 You could also use small willow hoops to make a frost flake (see Frisbees, page 92). Or you could lash together three sticks in the centre and stick small sticks onto these with masking tape.

5 Use short pieces of wool to hang nature finds from your frost flake, like feathers, pine cones and nuts.

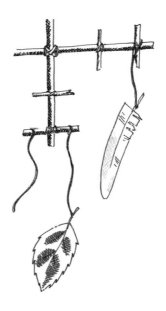

6 Did the weather forecast person say there might be frost tonight? If so, then tonight is the night to hang up your frost flake!

7 Tie a piece of string onto the top of your frost flake.

8 Find a place quite close to the ground to hang your flake.

This is where it will be coldest. Cover it with water and leave it for the night.

9 Go out first thing next morning, before the sun has warmed things up. Have you grown your own frost? Can you see how beautiful it is?

SNOWBALL TARGETS

Do you fancy doing something with snowballs that doesn't involve getting one in the face? With snowball targets you can have fun *with* your friends rather than against them. Throw to your heart's delight and rest assured you'll stay warm and dry.

COLLECT TOGETHER

From nature

☐ Long and short sticks, for different sizes of targets. Choose whatever you'd like.

From the Out Pack

☐ String
☐ Scissors

HOW TO MAKE IT

1 Lash (see skills section, page 140) three sticks of the same length together at the corners to make a triangle. This is a target.

2 Make more targets in many different sizes.

3 Place them on the ground, hang them from trees, put them on the wall.

4 Assign scores to each target and take turns with your friends to see who can get their snowballs through the targets.

5 After ten turns, who is the winner?

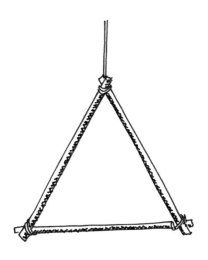

SKILLS

Skills are fantastic things to have. If you look after them, they will stay with you for the rest of your life.

They are not things you keep in a box or in your Out Pack, though. They are not heavy or soft or fragrant or loud. Skills are the wonderful things that you can learn to do with different parts of your body, sometimes just with your fingers and at other times with your arms, legs, teeth and eyebrows all at the same time! Can you zip up your coat, put on your shoes, or even tie up your laces? Those are all skills! So is being able to spot a pigeon, or a magpie, or tell which tree has acorns. The skills in this section will help you make whatever amazing things your imagination would like to create out of nature.

Have a look at the kite in our windy section. In the instructions it says to weave the grass. Well, when you learn how to weave it, you've learned a skill. And this is a wonderfully creative skill that people use to make fabrics and mats and baskets. You'll also get to learn about the warp and the weft; I can't think of anyone who wouldn't want to know about such funny-sounding things!

Skills are such useful things to have and I'm sure you'll enjoy learning them. But remember that they can sometimes be tricky to master, so don't worry if it's hard the first time that you do them. They need plenty of practice and you will probably discover that even your parents find them hard to do straight away.

FISH-ON-A-DISH KNOT

This is a fantastic knot that is useful for all sorts of things. It's just as it sounds: you put your fish on your dish and you've got it. And just in case you hear someone saying something about a clove hitch, don't worry, that's what grown-ups call a fish-on-a-dish knot. Not nearly as good!

COLLECT TOGETHER

☐ A stick
☐ String

HOW TO DO IT

1 Cut an arm's-length of string.

2 Hold the end of the string in your left hand.

3 Pinch the string with your right hand, slide it along the string a finger's-length and twist into a loop (this is the pinch-slide-twist). You have

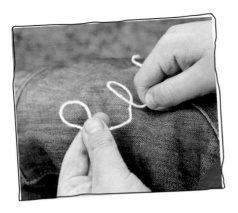 

now made your fish, and the fish's tail should bounce with your right hand.

4 Pinch the fish's tail quickly, before it swims away.

5 Pinch-slide-twist to the right of your fish to create the dish in just the same way.

6 Holding both your fish and your dish, put your fish on the dish by folding the loops together, slip both onto your stick and pull tight.

7 You have now created your fish-on-a-dish knot. Really well done!

LASHING

Lashing is a skill that Outpackers use all the time when they're creating in the outdoors. It's used to secure sticks together in a really strong way. Once you've learned how to lash, you'll be able to make a working water wheel, a weather vane that can actually tell you the direction of the wind and an awesome zipline hang-glider. And that's even before you start to think of all the fantastic things that you can invent yourself once you can lash two sticks together.

COLLECT TOGETHER

From nature
- [ ] Sticks

From the Out Pack
- [ ] String
- [ ] Scissors

HOW TO DO IT

1 Place the sticks you wish to lash next to each other.

2 First, tie your fantastic fish-on-a-dish knot onto the end of one of your sticks.

3 Take your string and weave it under and over your sticks – however many you wish to lash. This will fasten them together. Do this lots of times, leaving an arm's-length of string to tighten them.

4 Tighten the string in between the sticks by winding the tail-end of the string around the join. Secure with a knot. A granny knot is fine (see step 5). The fish-on-a-dish knot is hard to use when you're tying the end of the string.

5 A granny knot is when you tie one end of string to another end of string. Simply cross the two ends and pass one end under the other and pull tight. To complete the knot, cross the ends again and pass one under the other. Pull tight and this knot should hold.

6 Now get thinking – what else can you make now that you can lash sticks together?

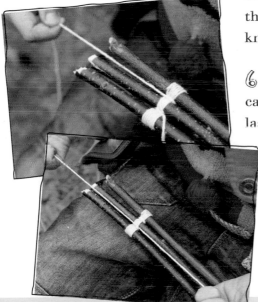

WEAVING

Weaving is a skill that people started using a very long time ago. Not quite when the cavemen were about, but there are signs that people were weaving about 27,000 years ago. So really, it's only right that we all know how to do it. Not to mention how beautiful it looks when you take long, luscious strands of grass and weave them together. And you can learn about the warp and the weft, right here!

HOW TO DO IT

1 First you need to make a weaving frame. It has to be fixed so that you have a frame to weave into, for example when you are weaving grass, stalks or reeds.

2 Cut a piece of masking tape: how long depends on how big you want your weaving to be. Lay it flat on the ground, sticky side up, from side to side. This is quite tricky because the tape sticks to your hands. Try using stones to keep the ends down.

3 Lay another piece of masking tape that is the same length on the ground, above the first one and parallel to it – the space in between the two pieces of tape should be a little shorter than whatever you are weaving.

4 Lay your grass, stalks or reeds from the bottom piece of tape to the top one, in a row. For grass, reeds and other wide materials, place them next to each other. If they're thinner like stalks or sticks, leave a small gap in between.

5 Keep going until you've placed all your materials along the masking tape. Now, wait for it – this bit is called the warp!

6 Lay another piece of masking tape over the top of each of the first pieces of masking tape, sticky side down, to secure the grass. This is your completed weaving frame. Now you are ready to weave. It's time for the weft!

7 Whatever you use to weave side to side through the warp is called the weft. Take a blade of grass (weft) and weave it under and over your taped grass (warp), until you reach the end.

8 Do this again, but this time go over and under. Continue this alternating pattern until you reach the other end.

9 Stick the loose ends of grass down with two more pieces of masking tape.

10 You should now have a woven grass square – or perhaps rectangle or diamond.

11 Can you think of anything else to make out of woven grass? Table mats, wall and garden decorations, a bookmark? You'll find it lasts for a long time, although it does shrink a bit – it's beautiful nonetheless.

HOW TO MAKE A STICK FRAME

If you want a stick weaving frame instead of using masking tape, make a square with four sticks and lash (see skills section, page 142) at the corners. To make the warp, tie lengths of wool from top to bottom and then weave through this with your weft.

WHAT WILL THE WEATHER DO NEXT?

People who study weather are called meteorologists. They use gauges and thermometers and barometers and anemometers and satellites to measure things like rain, wind, temperature and pressure. They look at what the weather is doing right now. Then they plug all the information into a computer to help them predict what the weather will do next. These days, this system is the most reliable way of making a weather forecast.

Sadly, we can't teach you how to do all that! What we can do is share a few clever ways to use the sky, the wind and the animals who live outdoors to help you guess what the weather might do next. None of these ways was figured out by us. Over thousands of years of living in this world of ever-changing weather, humans have noticed the patterns and have come up with some memorable sayings or proverbs about them. On the next page are some of our favourites.

WEATHER PROVERBS

The sky is full of magic. In our first book, *Let's Go Outside*, we talked about some of the clouds you might see, like cumulonimbus, cirrus, cumulus and nimbostratus. Aren't they fabulous names! Let's see what our age-old proverbs tell us about clouds...

Mackerel skies and mares' tails, Make tall ships take in their sails.

Mackerel skies are actually a cloud called an 'altocumulus'. It makes a spotty-dotty pattern that covers the whole sky and looks a bit like fish scales. Mares' tails are the cirrus clouds that are wispy and high up in the sky. When these two clouds are about, it tells us that some time that day a warm front is coming in that will bring with it some rain. So really those tall ships had better lower their big sails or they are going to be pushed about something terrible!

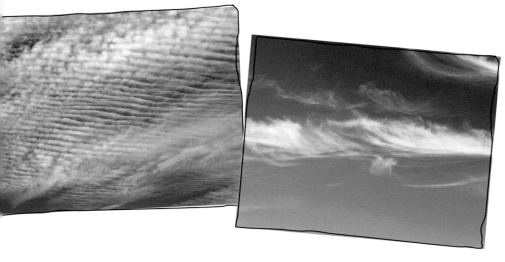

When clouds appear like rocks
and towers,
The earth's refreshed with
frequent showers.

This one is about the awesome cumulonimbus clouds, which we also know as thunderclouds. They look like gigantic rocks placed one on top of the other, making towers in the sky. There'll be some stormy weather when these are about.

Nimbostratus grey and wet,
There'll be some Outpacking
today, I bet!

I can't find a proverb about the grey rainy blanket, nimbostratus. So I've made one up myself.

WHAT THE WIND AND OTHER THINGS CAN TELL

If the clouds move against the wind, Rain will follow.

Have you ever looked up into the sky and seen the clouds moving in different directions – the big, fluffy cumulus clouds closer to the ground going one way and a grey sheet of altostratus clouds higher up going the other way? This can mean that rain and storms are on the way; there's a bit of a hodgepodge going on in the sky.

When dew is on the grass,
Rain will never come to pass.

Have you ever seen dewdrops on the grass even when it's a dry day? You walk on the grass and get wet feet. This kind of dew is more likely to form when the sky is clear and heat from planet Earth can rise up into space. It normally means that the rest of the day will be clear and sunny too. Although you never know, those mackerel skies and mares' tails might be on their way!

The sharper the blast,
The sooner it's past.

Did a rainstorm just blow in, seemingly out of nowhere? Chances are, the quicker the wind blows it in, the quicker it will blow it right back out again.

WHAT THE ANIMALS CAN TELL

Animals are much more in tune with the weather than we are, so watching their behaviour gives us all sorts of wonderful insights into what weather to expect next.

If the goose honks high, fair weather,
If the goose honks low, foul weather.

Have you ever heard honking and looked up to see geese flying in an arrow formation in the sky? Were they high in the sky or closer to the ground? When geese are flying high it means the weather is good. If they are closer to the ground the weather is bad, or will be soon. It all has to do with the air pressure in the atmosphere, which is called barometric pressure. Geese are clever at flying at a good height for the air pressure to help them speed along.

If spiders are many and
spinning their webs,
The spell will soon be very dry.

Rain can weigh spiders' webs down and can even break them, so if it's a bit moist outside the spiders will stay in bed and wait for a drier day to make their webs. When you see lots of spider's webs outside, you can expect a few dry days.

When seabirds fly to land,
There truly is a storm at hand.

Yes, spotting seabirds on land can tell us that there is a storm brewing out at sea. They would rather be on dry ground than stuck in the storm!

Next time you:

⛈ Spot freshly made spiders' webs

⛈ Notice a rainstorm blowing in quickly

⛈ See a sky full of altocumulus and
    cirrus clouds

Think of your proverbs and guess what the weather will do next.

WEATHER FORECAST

Welcome to today's weather update.

Today we are likely to see candyfloss clouds in the shapes of horses and velociraptors. These will pass over by noon and we will have a warm front emerging with friendly gusts of breeze. There may be the odd steamy shower that will help the brooks to babble and the flowers to sing. The evening will remain warm enough for running through sprinklers, barbecues and a touch of croquet. Watch out for tomorrow though; there be icy trolls about...

Have you ever seen the weather forecast on the TV? It probably looked like a map with lots of funny signs all over it. Perhaps a few drips and clouds or perhaps just great big suns all over the place! It's a very useful skill to have, being able to understand the weather forecast. Use our guide below the next time you're watching...you'll soon get the hang of it!

THE OUTPACKER'S GUIDE TO UNDERSTANDING A WEATHER FORECAST

Heavy rain: umbrella time!

Thunder and lightning: the tall clouds are doing a jig!

Sunny intervals: sun comes out, sun goes out, repeat!

Sun: light, bright and lovely!

Cloudy: mackerel skies and mares' tails – who's out today?

SO YOU'RE AN OUTPACKER!

You now know great and wonderful things about the natural world and the weather around you. You know about the seasons, the sky, about puddle ponies and how to make a relaxing place for a fairy to hang out in. This all makes you unbelievably special…this all makes you an Outpacker. So wherever you go – the park, the woods, your back yard or even the beach and the mountains – you can meet, make and imagine. You could have an Out Pack stay-and-play, an Out Pack weekend club or an Out Pack after-school club. There is plenty for you to do, and enough nature to keep you all making and imagining.

For even more ideas visit our website: www.theoutpack.co.uk

OTHER FUN STUFF TO SEE AND READ

Parents, grandparents and teachers, have a look at Project Wild Thing, a fantastic film-led movement to get more kids outside reconnecting with nature. Find it at player.bfi.org.uk/film/watch-project-wild-thing-2013

The National Trust's *50 Things to Do Before You're 11¾: An Outdoors Adventure Handbook* is a great list of 50 more ideas for things to do outdoors.

Have a look at the Woodland Trust (www.woodlandtrust.org.uk) and the Wildlife Trusts (www.wildlifetrusts.org). They always have an abundance of wonderful ideas for outdoor projects and activities in your local area.

INDEX

ACKNOWLEDGEMENTS

Thanks to Ben and Sophie, Izzy and Jess for trying out all of our ideas with yet more unquenchable enthusiasm. Thanks to both our amazing families for their continued support as we continue on this journey. Thanks to the staff at the Tamworth Snowdome, because however much we want it to, it doesn't snow in August! Thanks again to everyone at Pavilion Books for letting us do all this for a second time.

Steph would also like to acknowledge the invaluable help and support of Suzanne, Sarah, Zoe, Cheryl, Tamara, Cat, Tina, Anil and Jenny. For all the listening, compassion, expertise and tolerance, my most profound thanks.

ABOUT THE AUTHORS

Steph Scott is a speech and language therapist and scuba diving instructor. Katie Akers is a primary school teacher and forest school leader. They and their families have spent endless hours dashing through downpours, stomping through puddles and racing the wind to bring this book to life!